Learning
to Get
Along™

Understand and Care

Cheri J. Meiners, M.Ed.

Illustrated by Meredith Johnson

free spirit
PUBLISHING®

Library of Congress Cataloging-in-Publication Data
Meiners, Cheri J., 1957–
  Understand and care / Cheri J. Meiners ; illustrations by Meredith Johnson.
      p. cm.—(Learning to get along)
Summary: Explores how one can understand other people's feelings and how to be a good friend to someone who is feeling happy or sad.
  ISBN 1-57542-131-3
  1. Sympathy—Juvenile literature. 2. Empathy—Juvenile literature. [1. Sympathy. 2. Empathy. 3. Emotions. 4. Conduct of life.] I. Johnson, Meredith, ill. II. Title.
  BJ1475.M44 2003
  177'.7—dc21

                                                                    2003004007

Cover and interior design by Marieka Heinlen
Edited by Marjorie Lisovskis

Free Spirit Publishing Inc.
217 Fifth Avenue North, Suite 200
Minneapolis, MN 55401-1299

We're pleased to provide you with this book as an exclusive benefit of your membership in Thrivent Financial for Lutherans.

We understand what is important to you. Family. Faith. Giving back to your community and congregation. And achieving your financial goals. Our organization reflects *your* values in what we do.

To help you share your values with the children in your life, we are providing this book as a useful resource. If you would like to know more about the other member benefits available, ask your Thrivent Financial representative or reach us at one of the contact points below.

Thrivent Financial *for Lutherans*™

Where Values Thrive.™

4321 N. Ballard Road, Appleton, WI 54919-0001
www.thrivent.com • e-mail: mail@thrivent.com
800-THRIVENT (800-847-4836)

I have many different feelings.

Other people have many feelings, too.
I want to understand how other people feel.

When something happens to someone,

I can imagine how I would feel
if it happened to me.

Then I can understand
how someone else might feel.

I see my friend smile and laugh when she's happy.

She enjoys being with people and things she likes.

I understand how she feels.

I smile and laugh at some
of the same things.

When something nice happens
to someone,

I can remember times
when I have been happy.

I can imagine how I would feel.

Then I can understand how
the person feels.

I can show I care.

Someone I know may feel sad
when something goes wrong.

He may frown or cry.

I feel sad, too, when things go wrong for me.

I can imagine how I would feel
if the same thing happened to me.

I can understand how the person feels.
I can show I care.

Sometimes people feel angry
when things don't go the way they want.

Anger may show in a person's face, voice, or body.

I can remember feeling angry
when things didn't go my way.

I can try to understand how the person feels.
I can show I care.

If I'm not sure how someone is feeling,
I might ask, "How do you feel?"

Then I can listen.

Listening shows that I respect the person, and that I want to understand.

When I want to understand how someone feels,

I can watch how the person acts.
I can remember when I have felt that way.
I can imagine how I might feel.

I can ask and listen. I can show I care.

Understanding each other
helps us get along.

It feels good to understand and care!

Ways to Reinforce the Ideas in *Understand and Care*

As you read each page spread, ask children:

- What's happening in this picture?

Here are additional questions you might discuss:

Page 1

- What are feelings?

- What are some ways people in this picture are feeling? How can you tell?

Pages 2–5

- What does it mean to *imagine? (Children might suggest pretending or the idea of "make believe." As part of your conversation, you might discuss the idea of being in someone else's shoes—of pretending to be in someone's place and having the same experience and feelings.)*

- *(Point to child with spilled popcorn)* How would you feel if this happened to you? How do you imagine this child is feeling? Why do you think that?

Pages 6–7

- How are these children feeling? How can you tell?

- When are some times that you're happy?

- How does it feel to be happy? *(Include in your discussion other words for happy; children might suggest feelings like nice, good, excited, pleased, content, or joyful.)*

- How do you show that you're happy?

Pages 8–11

- *(Point to girl who kicked a goal)* Have you ever felt like this girl? What happened?

- How do you imagine she feels? How can you tell?

- How is the child showing the girl that he understands? What else could he do to let her know he cares?

Pages 12–17

- *(Point to boy who is eating alone)* How do you imagine this boy feels? How can you tell?

- Have you ever been sad? What are some things that make you sad?

- How does it feel to be sad? *(Include in your discussion other words for sad; children might suggest feelings like lonely, unhappy, blue, sorry, disappointed, or down.)*

- How do you show that you are sad?

- How is the child showing the boy that he cares? What else could he do to let him know he understands?

Pages 18–23

- *(Point to angry boy)* How do you imagine this boy feels? How can you tell? *(Focus discussion on the child who is angry. At some point you may also want to discuss how the child who inadvertently knocked down the blocks might be feeling as well.)*

- Do you remember a time when you felt angry? What happened?

- How does it feel to be angry? *(Include in your discussion other words for angry; children might suggest feelings like mad, grumpy, upset, furious, mean, or cranky.)*

- How do you show that you are angry?

- How is the child showing his brother that he understands? What else could he do to let him know he cares?

Pages 24–25

- How do you imagine this man feels? How can you tell? *(Accept all reasonable answers; it is not clear from the illustration exactly how the man is feeling.)*

- Can we always know how someone else feels? If you don't know, what can you do?

- What is respect? How does listening show respect? *(You might explain respect by saying, "When you show respect to people, you show that you think they are important.")* How does listening help us understand how someone feels?

- How do you know the boy is listening?

- What are some other questions you can ask to find out how someone is feeling? *(Some suggestions might include "What happened?," "Are you okay?," "Do you want to talk about it?")*

Pages 26–29

- *(Point to girl near dog)* How do you imagine this girl feels? How can you tell?

- How is the boy showing that he understands? How else could he show that he cares?

Pages 30–31

- Why do we want to understand how other people feel?

- What are some times when people might want us to understand and care? *(Help children realize that they can show understanding about all types of situations and feelings, including when people are excited, impatient, worried, confused, frustrated, and so forth.)*

Empathy Games

Understand and Care teaches empathy—a sincere, personal understanding of how another person feels. Here is a quick summary of the skills of empathy that are taught in the book:

1. Watch and listen to the person.

2. Remember when you have felt the same way.

3. Imagine how you might feel.

4. Ask what the person is feeling.

5. Show you care.

Read this book often with your child or group of children. Once children are familiar with the book, refer to it when teachable moments arise involving positive behavior or problems related to being empathic. Notice and comment when children show that they understand and care about how someone feels. Use the following activities to reinforce children's understanding of how to feel and show empathy.

Understanding Feelings

Preparation: Cut out pictures from magazines that show people in scenes where feelings are depicted. Glue the pictures to large index cards or card stock.

Level 1 *(reinforces Empathy Skill 1)*

Hold up a card and point to the picture. Ask, "What's happening?" Then ask, "How does the person feel? How can you tell?" As needed, discuss and explain what's happening or how someone is feeling.

Level 2 *(reinforces Empathy Skills 1 and 5)*

Using dolls, action figures, stuffed animals, or puppets, role-play a scenario discussed in Level 1. Begin by using the props yourself and enacting the scene while children watch. Then ask questions like the following: "How does Strong Man feel?" "How could LuLu Duck show him she understands?" After children suggest ideas, have children use the dolls or puppets to act out the scenes, showing understanding and caring.

My Feelings Book *(reinforces Empathy Skill 2)*

Materials: Drawing paper, crayons or markers, pencils or pens, colored construction paper, hole punch, and yarn

Preparation: Prepare pages and covers for feelings books. At the top of each sheet of drawing paper, write the name of a different feeling (examples: happy, sad, angry, surprised, scared, proud, excited, jealous, thankful). On the construction paper, write "My Feelings Book." You will want to have a cover and a complete set of sheets labeled with the feelings for each child. Plan to complete this activity over several sessions.

Talk with children about one of the emotions, using questions like these: "What are some times when people might feel proud? Can you remember a time when you felt proud? What happened?" Then invite children to draw pictures of a time when they were proud. Also have children write (or dictate for you to write) a sentence explaining their pictures. Repeat this activity for other emotions. Have children write their names on the covers and decorate them if they wish. Use the hole punch and yarn to bind the books.

Imagining How I Might Feel

Preparation: On index cards, write individual scenarios similar to the following. Place the cards in a bag.

Sample Scenarios:

- Children on the bus were calling Willie names.
- Maureen just learned how to ride a two-wheel bike by herself.
- Lakisha's friend was invited to a party, but Lakisha wasn't invited.
- Carlo is starting a new school, and two children asked him to play with them.
- A child walked by and messed up the puzzle Rufus was putting together.

Level 1 *(reinforces Empathy Skill 3)*

Have a child draw a card. Read or have a child read it aloud. Say, "Imagine this happened to you. How would you feel? How do you think the person feels?" Continue having children draw cards and discuss scenarios.

Level 2 *(reinforces Empathy Skill 5)*

After playing Level 1, have children draw and read the cards again, one by one. This time ask, "How could you show you understand (care)?" If needed, offer examples, appropriate and inappropriate, and have children choose: "Willie feels sad because some children were calling him names. How would you show Willie you care? Would you call the other kids names? Would you ask Willie to sit with you? Which would show you care?" Continue discussing scenarios, encouraging a variety of appropriate ways to show understanding and caring.

Understanding Feelings Dice Roll *(reinforces Empathy Skills 1–5)*

Materials: Cards prepared for "Understanding Feelings" activity (page 34), one standard dice, whiteboard or poster paper, and marker

Write the five numbered skills on the whiteboard or poster paper. As you do, briefly explain and review each skill with children. Ask a child to start the game by drawing a picture card out of the bag and rolling the dice. The number on the dice corresponds with the skill number. For example, if a child rolls a two, point to skill 2 and ask question 2, below. (If a six is rolled, the child can choose which skill to talk about.) Continue playing until each child has had one or more turns and all the skills have been discussed. If you like, use language and questions like the following in discussing the skills:

1. Look at the person's face (mouth, body). How does the person look? (What do you think the person is saying? How is the person acting?)

2. Can you remember a time when something like this happened to you? What happened? How did you feel?

3. Imagine this happened to you. How would you feel? (Why?)

4. What could you ask to find out how the person feels?

5. What could you say or do to show you care?